Pueblo Stories

& Storytellers

by MARK BAHTI

TREASURE CHEST BOOKS: TUCSON, ARIZONA

Treasure Chest Books
P. O. Box 5250
Tucson, AZ 85703-0250
(520) 623-9558

ISBN 1-887896-01-5
Library of Congress No. 96-61115

This book is set in Centaur and Schneidler
Edited by Linnea Gentry
Designed by Paul Mirocha
Printed in Korea

Photo credits:
Michel Monteaux, from the Girard Foundation Collection, Museum of International
Folk Art, Museum of New Mexico, Santa Fe: page 8
Robin Stancliff: front cover, half title, title spread, contents page, pages 13, 15, 16,
17, 18. 19, 28, 29, 31, 34, 35, 38, 53, 56, and back cover
David Burckhalter: pages 9, 10, 11, 14, 20, 22, 24, 25 26, 32, 33, 39, 43, 42, 43

ACKNOWLEDGMENTS

Many people are due a large measure of thanks for assisting in the creation of this book and in its recent revision.

Alexander Anthony, Jr., Bill Beaver, Bob Gallegos, Chuck Hall, and John Kennedy, Sr., provided an excellent selection of storyteller figurines to photograph. Chris and Vera Fragua as well as Corinne Garcia of Acoma were very helpful in providing special examples of their work for inclusion in this volume. My thanks, also, to Eleanore Voutselas, manager of Archival Collections of the Museum of International Folk Art.

Photographers David Burckhalter (first edition) and Robin Stancliff (revised edition) went about their work professionally, efficiently, and with good humor.

Editors Dolores Rivas Bahti (first edition) and Linnea Gentry (second edition) kept the text flowing and my syntax intact.

But the greatest measure of thanks goes to those who still tell the stories and those who still listen.

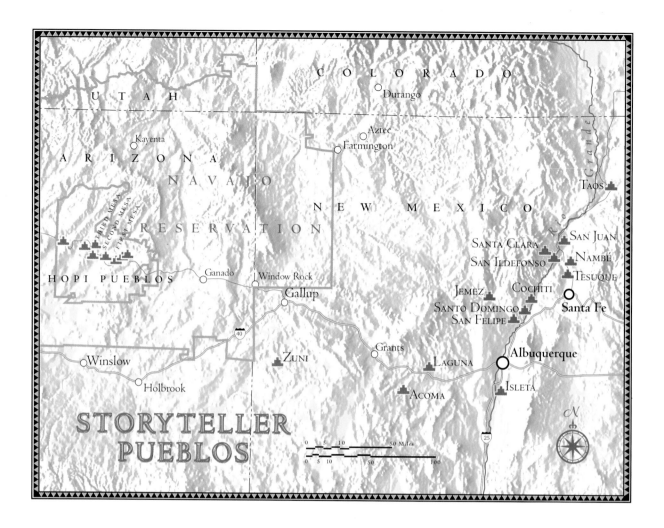

STORYTELLER
PUEBLOS

Contents

Vera Fragua

JEMEZ

Storyteller Beginnings

MANY OF THE PUEBLO INDIANS of New Mexico have a tradition of figurative pottery that is best known from collections begun in the 1880s. Most of these were single figures of individuals, both Indian and non-Indian. They were not religious in nature despite names that often imply otherwise. A notable example is the (in)famous 'Tesuque Rain God,' which was commissioned by a midwestern candy manufacturer as part of a promotion. It had nothing to do with Tesuque religion or rain gods, having apparently been inspired by figurines from Mexico. The figurine of the Singing Mother, a female holding a single child, seems to date back to about the turn of the century, and Singing Mothers are still being made today.

opposite page:
Helen Cordero, COCHITI

below:
Helen Cordero, COCHITI

The first true storyteller figure did not appear until 1964, when a well-known collector of folk art, Alexander Girard, encouraged potter Helen Cordero of Cochiti Pueblo to expand upon the mother and child concept. She eventually made a figure of a Pueblo man with five children on his lap and shoulders, inspired by and made in memory of her remarkable grandfather, Santiago Quintana.

Quintana was a Cochiti elder who had followed the ancient tradition of maintaining his village's culture through storytelling. A man of great vision, Quintana also recognized the value of working with ethnologists and anthropologists and for over forty years, beginning in the 1880s, helped to create a permanent written record of those same stories.

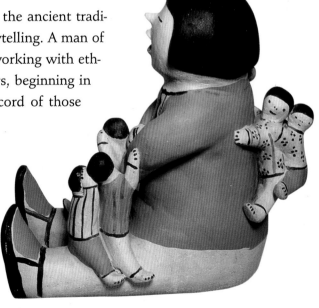

It has been more than half a century since the children gathered around him to hear yet another story from this gifted storyteller, and the grandchildren who listened to him and learned from him now have their own grandchildren. But the man and what he devoted much of his life to preserving have not faded from memory, nor are they likely to.

Working with the Clay

ACCORDING TO MOST RIO GRANDE PUEBLO TRADITIONS, clay is considered a living substance. In some villages, potters offer prayers and cornmeal as they gather Mother Clay. Trips for clay may also include gathering plants and minerals used to make paint. Potsherds, sand, or volcanic tuff may also be collected for use as a temper to promote quick and thorough drying and to prevent the clay from cracking.

After collection, the clay is set in the sun to dry. It is then soaked in buckets of water for up to four days, after which the water is poured off

 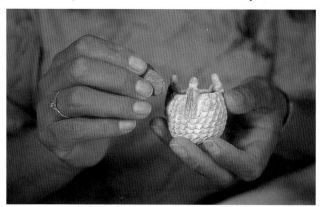

and fresh water added until it runs clear. More water is added as the potter stirs the clay and breaks up any remaining lumps by hand. The clay is poured through a sieve to remove pebbles, twigs, and other foreign matter. After the excess water has evaporated or been poured off, the temper is added. In addition to aiding the drying process, the temper also makes the clay less sticky and easier to work, once the strenuous task of mixing and kneading the temper and clay is done.

Potters do not usually measure the ingredients but rely instead on 'feel' to determine if it is right. When the mixture is ready, the clay is wrapped in plastic to prevent further drying.

To model a storyteller, potters generally use a paddle and anvil technique, as the form does not lend itself to the traditional coiling method used in forming jars and bowls. The pieces of clay are pinched and added together to build the body. The potter takes care to join each piece to the

growing figure securely and smoothly so that no air pockets destroy it during firing. Using a piece of gourd or small wedge of cottonwood, the potter scrapes and sands the figure until smooth and then leaves it to dry. If it cracks, it goes back into a bucket of water to dissolve. And the potter then begins anew. If all goes well, the next stage begins.

In this phase, a clay slip is applied to the figure. At many pueblos, the slip is smoothed and polished with a stone. Potters have a variety of these stones, each a different shape for different surfaces. They may have been found in streambeds, bought at rock shops, or handed down through several generations of potters. When the slip is finished, the paint work begins. Potters traditionally use mineral and vegetal paints, with various types of clay, hematite, ochre, and beeweed being the most commonly used pigments. A few potters apply clay paints or acrylic paints after the firing process.

The figurines are fired in one of two ways. Potters may use gas or electric kilns, which can bake at temperatures 500 to 1,000 degrees higher than traditional firing techniques. The traditional method uses wood, coal, or animal dung for fuel, is done in the kiln out of doors, and carries with it a number of risks. If the ground is too damp, if a wind springs up, if it rains, or if the weather changes in any significant fashion, the potter may lose the work. A poorly constructed piece can literally blow up, taking with it the other pieces in the kiln. Even a poorly laid fire can ruin the work by creating smudges or fireclouds or by incompletely firing or cracking the work, should the heat rise too quickly.

New ideas and techniques enrich old traditions as craftspeople continue to work with clay. They remember, as at Cochiti, the admonition of Clay Old Woman: Never forget to make pottery!

Corrine Garcia making storytellers
ACOMA

Storytelling

CENTURIES AGO, AN ELDER BEGAN A STORY, speaking in a dimly lit room in a pueblo cloaked in the starlit vastness of a winter night. During those long nights when the earth, plants, animals, and people were quiet, awaiting the sun's return, storytelling was a significant part of village life.

Many stories could be told only during this time, when one was safe from lightning and the snakes slept. Young ones would gather around to listen to an elder, usually a man, tell a story. They were admonished to sit up straight and listen carefully.

Though these story times no longer occur so often, many Pueblo people remember those nights and keep the stories alive. Both the stories and the storyteller figurines commemorate and celebrate this tradition. Storytelling sessions begin after the evening meal. It may be part of the Creation Story, a recounting that requires many such nights; or it might be a story about how Coyote scattered the stars or a personal reminiscence of a hunting trip. But whether it happened in the days when cars were new or when the world itself was new, the stories have a power to hold their listeners. The old ones tell the stories as they heard them when they were young from the old ones who had heard them in turn from the old ones before them. Each generation saw to it that the oral traditions were passed on, virtually unchanged, for uncounted years.

The adults—aunts, uncles, mothers, and fathers—would quietly work or sit and listen, for the telling was neither ritual nor entertainment, poetry nor prose. Rather, it was all these things and more, much more. As the storyteller wove his tale, he was also knitting a new generation into its long past, maintaining a cultural tapestry in a way that the most advanced printing, computer, or video technology has yet to match.

Stories such as those accompany the photographs of the pottery storytellers in this book. They are largely folktales. Versions of most of these stories can be found in the anthologies listed in the reading list at the end of this book. Religious material, such as the emergence or creation stories, have not been included. This is because traditional religious leaders in many pueblos have expressed concern about making them public, a concern ranging from discomfort to outright complete opposition to recording or further disseminating such material. This protective attitude is understandable considering that their religions were officially suppressed, even banned, from Spanish colonial times up until 1934, when religious freedom was finally extended to America's original inhabitants. In recent years a desire to romanticize and emulate Indian cultures has resulted in another threat: trivializing traditional beliefs and practices and removing their power and mystery by taking them out of their culture and out of context.

The stories are meant to be told out loud, not read. So read them aloud, slowly. Measure your words against the story and find its rhythm. Give the stories plenty of thought and time in the telling. Let the words begin to paint the picture. Repeat a line that needs repeating—quietly—or perhaps loudly! Feel the story. And when you are finished, you may want to recall and reclaim some of the stories that are a part of your own heritage.

For those interested in reading more traditional Indian stories and learning more about the living cultures which have nurtured and preserved them, an annotated bibliography at the end of the book contains many reliable sources.

Mary Small, LAGUNA

Detail

Tiwa Pueblos

ISLETA

Isleta Pueblo is known to its people as Tuei (too-EH). Most of the nearly 3,700 members still live on their 211,000-acre reservation located just south of Albuquerque. When the Spanish came to the area, there were twenty southern Tiwa (TEE-wah) villages. The Spanish authorities consolidated them to ease the task of governing, and by the late 1700s Isleta was the sole southern Tiwa village. The Tigua Pueblo of El Paso identify themselves as Tiwas who were forced to accompany the Spanish when they fled the upper Rio Grande area during the Great Pueblo Revolt of 1680. Following a bitter dispute at the Keres pueblo of Laguna in the late 1870s, many people left Laguna and settled at Isleta. Much of what is known as Isleta pottery is made by descendants of the Laguna colony.

It remains a conservative village in many respects. At Isleta, folktales like the one that follows are called "pa-ishe" (pah-EEH-sheh). To prevent the sacred stories from being told to outsiders, pueblo members are cautioned from youth that if they tell them to strangers, their lives will be shortened.

Evelyn Concho, TAOS

TAOS

The name Taos is derived from the Tiwa word tua (TU-ah), which means "houses." The pueblo is divided in half, with the Taos River separating North House from South House. The Spanish first visited this pueblo in 1540, establishing a mission there in the early 1600s. Unhappy with Spanish rule, the people left Taos and built a pueblo far to the east, in what is now Kansas. Two years later the Spanish coaxed them back to New Mexico. Taos Pueblo is located just north of the town which bears the same name. Picuris is the other northern Tiwa pueblo. Located south of Taos, Picuris does not currently produce storytellers, though there are a number of fine potters in the village.

Like Isleta, Taos is a conservative pueblo, with the secular officers chosen by five religious leaders. There are over 4,400 tribal members, of whom about two-thirds live on their 95,000-acre reservation. Traditional pottery from this village is made with a mica-flecked clay that gives it a golden sheen.

It Takes an Old Man

HA! THE PEOPLE DECIDED THEY NEEDED A LEADER, a t'ai-kabehdeh. But they did not know how to find the right man, or how to make him a leader when they found him. They didn't even know the ceremonies, so they went without food and water for four days while they thought about this.

They decided to call upon a boy in the village. They did not like this boy. They called him 'Big Head,' but he was smart and they thought he might know something.

The boy told them that they had once had a leader, at the beginning, but he had been left behind when they entered this world. The people asked Big Head to bring their old leader to this world. Since the boy had so much power, he agreed to do this.

He went away for twelve days. When he returned he brought the old t'aikahbehdeh, who then told the people how to find a new leader. And he told them how to pick the other leaders they would need. When the people had chosen the new leader, the old one told the new one how to do things. "You must look after your people. All of your time must be spent doing this. You must not work at other things or kill anything—even an insect. You must stay inside and pray and make ceremonies," he said. Then the old one left to go back to the other world.

The new leader found it hard to stay inside and not work or hunt or plant or dance. One day he went to chop wood. Nothing happened to him, so he decided the rule could be broken.

Stella Teller, ISLETA

Later, when he was outside hunting, he heard a voice. It was the voice of the old t'aikahbehdeh saying, "You did not respect me. You did not do as I said." And though the disobedient young t'aikahbehdeh could not see a whip, he felt it on his back.

The new leader was told to go back and tell the people, "Never elect a young t'aikahbedeh again, only an old man. Young men have too many ideas." The old t'aikahbehdeh said, "They will not mind or serve the people like old men will."

The young leader returned to his village and gave the people the old man's message. After telling it, he died. And that is why only an old man can be a t'aikahbehdeh.

Kau eh kyen.

Towa Pueblos

JEMEZ

When the Spanish entered northern New Mexico, there were eleven small, Towa-speaking villages which they forcibly consolidated into two, Jemez and Pecos. The Towa Indians vigorously opposed the Spanish for many years, even attacking pueblos which they considered to be supportive of the Spanish. They finally settled peacefully at the site of the present village in 1703. The surviving inhabitants of the other village, Pecos, joined them in 1838.

Jemez is known as Walatoa (wah-LA-toe-ah) to its residents. Nearly two-thirds of their more than 2,600 members live on their 89,000-acre reservation, located at the foot of the Jemez Mountains west of Santa Fe, New Mexico. This is only a small portion of their traditional lands. A story at Jemez warns the Jemez people that should they forget or neglect to do as instructed and leave the old ways, Father Sun would take away all their lands and give them to someone else. Father Sun also told them that if such a thing came to pass, when they came back to the old ways, he would "return on the wings of the morning sun and banish the intruders and restore your lands."

Traditional potterymaking declined and virtually disappeared at Jemez in this century. However, in the late 1970s a dramatic reversal began. The sun-dried, poster-paint ware has been replaced by handmade, often traditionally fired pottery and clay sculpture.

Chris Fragua, JEMEZ

The Twins and the Giant

DIH PALOH.

IN THOSE TIMES AND IN THAT PLACE, the people were unhappy and afraid. A giant, Tsakapi'yadya, roamed the land, capturing and eating people. He also kept all the game animals for himself. Nearby lived twin boys who had great power. The people asked the boys to help them and the twins agreed. For four days the twins purified themselves. After the four days had passed, they gathered their bows and arrows and throwing sticks and went to the village plaza to dance and sing their songs. The people of the village joined them, dancing and singing also and then going with them on their way to where Tsakapi'yadya lived. But when they were halfway there, the boys told the people to go back to the village and wait. So the people returned.

The twins continued their journey and soon arrived where Tsakapi'yadya lived. They were still singing. Tsakapi'yadya heard them and came to greet them in a friendly and kind way. But the twins paid no attention to him. He complimented them for their fine singing. Still they ignored him. Then he told them that they must be very brave and very strong, and if they were, they should play a game with him. At this they stopped singing and agreed to his invitation.

"First we must eat," said Tsakapi'yadya. And so saying he brought out great amounts of many foods. There was boiled corn, great steaming bowls of beans, heaps of venison, baskets filled with dried rabbit meat, squash, melon. More food than their people had ever seen, but the twins ate only a little venison. Tsakapi'yadya ate a great deal. In fact, he ate everything!

When they were done, Tsakapi'yadya spoke again, saying, "We will take our bows and arrows and see who can send an arrow to that far mountain in the south." He paused and then added, "And we will bet our lives."

The smaller twin spoke, saying, "You might as well kill us now, for we cannot shoot that far." But the giant insisted they try, for had they not agreed to play the game? "Very well," said the larger twin, "but you must shoot first."

DEE-pah-lo

tsa-KA-pee-YA-dja

Mary Small, LAGUNA

So the giant shot first, with his huge bow and arrow made from a pine tree. The arrow flew far and landed at the base of the mountain. The giant was very pleased. Very pleased. Then the twins shot their arrows. First the smaller twin shot and then the larger twin shot. Both arrows flew over the mountain and beyond! When Tsakapi'yadya saw this he said, "I am finished then. I die."

He wanted to eat again before he died, and this the twins allowed. After he had eaten, they went out into the canyon. There he gave them his club of petrified wood so that they might kill him with it. But the twins refused, saying they would use instead a small piece of petrified wood they had brought with them. The giant objected, saying they could not possibly kill him with so small an object. But they struck him with it and he died instantly. His body fell into the canyon and broke into many pieces.

The twins then ran to where Tsakapi'yadya kept the people he had captured and planned to eat. They freed the people and also the animals that he had kept locked up. So the people went home to their villages, and the animals went home to their mountains. The people were very glad and said, "Now we shall have a happy life!"

keh-TSAY-dah-ba 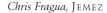   K'tsedaba.

Chris Fragua, Jemez

Chris and Vera Fragua, JEMEZ

The Great Serpent

AT PECOS PUEBLO the people were in a time of great need. The rain had failed. Their crops had failed. And the animals of the forest had left. There was a dryness and great heat upon the land.

Pen-yu, a great serpent, appeared and spoke to them, saying, "I will help you, but in return, you must honor me." The people quickly agreed.

True to his word, he gave the people food. He gave them water. He called the animals back to the forests and the rain back to their fields. The people, in turn, made prayer offerings to him. But Pen-yu told the people that he would care for them always, providing they sacrificed a small boy to him at each passing of the moon. "If you do not do this for me," he threatened and thundered, "things will be as before and worse!"

The people were unhappy and afraid. No one knew what to do. Finally a man came forth and spoke. He advised the people to defy Pen-yu. He offered to help protect the people with his medicine power. He asked nothing in return. The people agreed to defy Pen-yu and accepted the man's offer.

When Pen-yu did not receive his offering at the passing of the next moon, he became very angry. He demanded his sacrifice. The people again refused and so he attacked them. But he could not hurt them, for their new medicine was too strong. He left in a great rage, carving out arroyos with his thrashing tail as he stormed away.

Rose DeVore, JEMEZ

Tewa Pueblos

SANTA CLARA

Santa Clara is the name the Spanish gave to the village of Kha'po. The present village was built in the 1300s. After the Great Pueblo Revolt of 1680, many people went west to live with the Hopi. Although some later moved back, the Tewa village of Hano still remains at Hopi, maintaining the Tewa language and customs.

Roughly two-thirds of Santa Clara Pueblo's 9,600 members live on nearly 46,00 acres of reservation land along the Rio Grande, immediately south of Española, New Mexico. Like many pueblos, there was a split between those willing to accept federal programs and rules and those who wished to maintain the traditional ways. In 1935 Santa Clara became the first village to adopt a tribal constitution, setting up a secular government with elected officials and leaving the traditional leaders to direct the religious life of the pueblo.

Santa Clara is famous for its painted, carved, and polished black and redware pottery. Some polychrome ware is also produced. There are over 100 individuals who make pottery, but it is a full-time occupation for only a handful.

SAN ILDEFONSO

Called Pohogeh Oweengeh (po-HO-geh o-WEEN-geh), Village Where the River Cuts Down Through, San Ildefonso lies just south of Santa Clara. After moving to their present village site after the Great Pueblo Revolt, they suffered a series of disasters, including a smallpox outbreak that killed half of the population in the late 1700s and the influenza outbreak in 1918. The latter dropped their population to less than one hundred. Factionalism arising from the moving of the village and its main plaza to just north of its old location created deep divisions that affected both the religious and civil authority of the village for decades.

The world-famous, world-class potter Maria Martinez lived here until her death. She and her husband, Julian, are credited with helping to revive the now-famous style of pottery with matte black on polished blackware. The village produces the same range of pottery types as Santa Clara. Their 26,000-acre reservation is home to nearly 1,500 members.

NAMBÉ

Nambé has the distinction of being known by its native name, which means 'Mound of Earth.' Approximately 600 tribal members have a 19,000-acre reservation north of Santa Fe, New Mexico. Heavily intermarried with descendants of the early Spanish colonists, it was once predicted that this pueblo would eventually lose all of its Tewa Indian identity. The revival of traditional ceremonial life, which has touched most Rio Grande pueblos, has also affected Nambé and strengthened its identity.

Manuel Vigil, TESUQUE

TESUQUE

Tesuque (teh-SU-kay) is a Spanish corruption of the native name Tet-su-geh, meaning 'cottonwood tree place.' Many of its 400 members live on their 17,000-acre reservation. Theirs was the first village to strike during the revolt in 1680. They abandoned the village shortly thereafter and did not return until the early 1700s. More conservative than some of the other Tewa villages, the secular leaders are chosen each year by the religious leaders of the village.

Pottery making declined about the turn of the century, with most work limited to pieces that were sun-dried rather than fired and then decorated with poster paints.

SAN JUAN

Also known as Okeh, San Juan was established about 1300 AD. Tribal enrollment is about 1,600, nearly half of whom live on the 12,000-acre reservation north of Española, New Mexico, along the Rio Grande River. As at Tesuque, the religious leaders select the secular leaders each year.

The first Spanish capitol of New Mexico was established here, the largest of all the Tewa pueblos. Ironically, the leader of the Pueblo Revolt that drove out the Spanish was from San Juan.

The Man Who Was Turned into a Witch

A MAN AND HIS WIFE LIVED TOGETHER. He was a good and honest man, a good husband, and a good hunter. Every four days he would bring a deer to his wife. He had a friend who went with him to hunt. His friend loved his wife and his wife loved his friend more than she loved her husband. Soon his friend and his wife made plans to get rid of him.

It happened that the friend was a witch. He told the man's wife that he knew how to get rid of the husband. He made a special large hoop with his magic. Then he called his witch companions, and they visited the husband. When they arrived, they invited the husband to do a dance with them and practice that night. The husband didn't want to, so one of the witchboys told the man he should come and watch and listen, since it was a new kind of dance. So the husband agreed.

On the way, one of the witches suggested they steal a chicken. Another asked how they could do it without being noticed. The first replied that he had a hoop with which they could turn themselves into coyotes. "I shall show you how," he said.

He rolled the hoop, and as he ran through it, he became a coyote! They rolled it again, and as he ran back through it, he became a man again! Each witchboy took a turn running through the hoop to become a coyote and back again to change into a man. When the husband's turn came, he ran through and was turned into a coyote, too. But the hoop disappeared before he could change back. They had destroyed it! The witchboys laughed at him and began to chase him.

The poor, frightened man ran to his house and scratched at the door with his paw until his wife appeared. She was startled to see a coyote and called for help. The witchboys came running with their bows and arrows. To keep from being killed, the coyote had to run away and hide in his brother's cornfield.

The next morning his brother saw the coyote and set his dogs on him. When the dogs came near enough to smell him, they wagged their tails and didn't chase him or bite him.

"Do not shoot that coyote, Grandson," said his grandmother, "for he may be your brother."

Dorothy and Paul Gutierrez
SANTA CLARA

Margaret and Luther Gutierrez
SANTA CLARA

"If you are my brother, then come here beside me." The coyote walked forward miserably and sat down beside his brother.

"Are you truly a coyote?" his brother asked. The coyote began to cry and nod his head. Then his brother and grandmother cried and took him home.

His parents cried when they saw what had happened to their son. They called his wife, but when he saw her, the coyote chased her out of the house. The family called the White Corn Medicine Men. They worked four days, but by the fourth day they were still not able to change him back into a man.

They called on the Black Corn Medicine Men, who tried for four days to change him back. They, too, failed.

Then they asked the Blue Corn Medicine Men, who tried for four days. But they, too, failed.

They then asked the Yellow Corn Medicine Men to try. But after four days, they also failed.

Finally they asked the Many-Colored Corn Medicine Men of the Middle Place to help them. "You must bring your brother's best friend to stay while we work for four days to save him," they said. They told the brother to take the coyote along so he could show him which friend to bring.

When they arrived at the friend's house, he said he was sick and could not go with them. So they dragged him back to the place where the Many-Colored Corn Medicine Men waited for them. "But," he said, "the hoop was burned." Still, the Many-Colored Corn Medicine Men made him stay for four days. On the morning of the fourth day, the witchboy agreed to make a new hoop and change the coyote back into a man. "But only if you spare my life," he bargained. The Many-Colored Corn Medicine Men replied that it was up to him if he lived or died, not them.

The night of the fourth day, a new hoop was ready. The coyote went through it four times. First his head changed back into that of a man. His arms changed back on his second time through the hoop. Then his body changed on the third passage. On the fourth time, his legs and feet changed and he was as he had been.

They gave the hoop back to the witchboy and told him to leave. When he returned home, he burned the hoop.

The witch died of shame before morning.

The Maiden and the Turkeys

A MOTHER AND A FATHER DIED, and their young daughter was taken into the family of her mother's sister, as is the custom. Her aunt had many children, so she did not want another child to feed. In time she began to mistreat her niece. When the girl was but six years old, she was given the task of tending the flock of turkeys the family owned.

Each morning she led them from their pens into the canyon to feed. Each night she brought them back and penned them up again. She was often sent out before breakfast and without a lunch, even without corn-cakes to eat. When she returned at nightfall, she was told many times that supper was over and she had missed the evening meal.

The turkeys took pity on her for she was very kind to them. When they went into the canyon, they gathered feed for her. They brought all types of berries. They brought her piñons and acorns. And they taught her their language. They combed and untangled her hair with their beaks and spun their feathers to mend her clothes.

Since she was gone during the day and returned only towards dark, few people in the village saw her or knew much about her. Some people called her the Turkey Maiden, but mostly they ignored her. Even the young men in the village paid her no attention.

One night she heard the excited conversation between her girl cousins about a social dance that would bring many people from the surrounding villages. The girls busied themselves laying out their best clothes and finest

Margaret and Luther Gutierrez
SANTA CLARA
Tewa Clowns

shell and turquoise jewelry for the dance. But the Turkey Maiden did not enter into the preparations for she knew that she had nothing to wear but her torn and patched manta (woven dress). She could not endure the laughter and pointing and whispers that an appearance in such clothes would bring. The next morning, on the way to the canyon she confided the cause of her great and growing sadness to her turkey companions. Her sadness filled their hearts with sorrow. So that night the turkeys made a plan.

The girl rose earlier than usual the day of the dance to be well away from the village before the people arrived and the dance began. As the girl reached the canyon, the turkeys stopped and gathered around her.

"Strike us with this juniper limb," one of the turkeys instructed. The girl protested that she would not do anything to harm her friends. Four times they asked her and four times she refused. So they rushed at her as if to attack. This frightened her so much that she picked up the stick and struck at them.

From under the wing of the first turkey fell a new and beautiful manta. From the second fell a wonderful red, green, and black sash. From the third fell gleaming white buckskin moccasins. And from the fourth fell necklaces of turquoise and shell,

"You must allow us to bathe you and arrange your hair. Then put on these garments and return to the village. But while you enjoy the dance, do not forget us. Be sure you return to the canyon before dark," they said. The Turkey Maiden readily agreed and promised she would never forget her friends.

She went happily to the village and contentedly noticed that though no one recognized her as the Turkey Maiden, everyone looked at her admiringly. The young men came to speak to her, and the women wondered where the maiden had come from. Her day was spent so well that all thought of her loyal friends and companions flew from her mind. Only after dark did she finally remember. Frightened and sorrowful, she left the plaza and ran to the canyon.

But the turkeys were not there. They had left and were scattered throughout the canyon and up into the mountains. She called to them, but they ignored her.

She ran after them, as they had taught her to run, but they ran faster. To this day the turkeys are spread out over the canyons and mountains. And to this day they do not trust people, but flee from them.

Marilyn Henderson, ACOMA

Keresan Pueblos

ACOMA

The mesa-top village of Acoma (AH-ko-mah) sits on a 378,000-acre reservation with several satellite communities in central New Mexico. Two-thirds of the tribes 5,000 members live there. The present village was built about 1150 AD.

Prior to Spanish contact, the Acoma people lived in several villages in the region. Relations with the Spanish invaders, rocky at best, worsened when soldiers demanded tribute and supplies. The soldiers were killed, after which the Spanish military responded by laying siege to the village and destroying their fields. Eventually their mesa-top pueblo was overcome. Women survivors over the age of twelve were sentenced to hard labor for twenty-five years. Men over twenty-five received the same punishment in addition to having a foot chopped off. Young girls were given to the Church and the boys to the officer who led the siege.

Remarkably, Acoma managed to survive, though to this day visitors are closely regulated and can enter only with a guide. The village is closed to all outsiders during religious observances. Acoma pottery is known for its thin walls and intricate designs executed in black (or sometimes red-brown) on white.

COCHITI

Cochiti (KO-chee-tee), a mispronunciation of the native name of Kot'yeteh, is a village resting on about 50,000 acres of land south of Santa Fe on the Rio Grande. Half of its 1,300 members live in or near the village. The village was settled in 1250 AD as a result of a split between two factions in a larger, now-abandoned pueblo. The other village formed was San Felipe.

For fourteen years after the 1680 revolt, Cochiti was abandoned. The residents had retreated to the fortified settlement of Cieneguilla, along with refugees from Taos, San Felipe, Picuris, and Santo Domingo. The Spanish destroyed Cieneguilla during the reconquest, and the people of Cochiti returned to their old village.

Helen Cordero, who made the first storyteller figurine, was from Cochiti. The pueblo is also famous for fine, large drums.

Kasewats and the Giantess

KAH-say-wats

SKO-yo

Judy Suina, COCHITI

KASEWATS WENT HUNTING. He didn't have any luck hunting, so he knew something was not right with his wife. That is how it is for a hunter. When he returned home he did not see his wife, but his mother told him the story of what had happened.

His wife had gone to the spring that morning to fill her water jar. While there, a sko'yo , or giantess, had snatched her up. At this time many giants and monsters still lived near their village of A'sko. They roamed about carrying huge baskets on their backs. In the baskets they placed the people they caught to cook and eat.

Kasewats left immediately to track the sko'yo but soon lost the trail in a storm. So that night he made a plan. The next day he went to the spring and made much noise but made no attempt to conceal himself. Thus it was that the sko'yo was able to catch him as well. She carried him west to her home. She lived near the highest peak in the Zuni Mountains. There he was put into a room where he found his wife and many others who were very frightened. The sko'yo was fattening them up before cooking them.

When the sko'yo began to heat some rocks to cook a stew, Kasewats called out to her, "Who are you going to eat next, miserable one?" This made the sko'yo very angry, and she grabbed him up, shouting, "You!" She began to wash him before throwing him into the pot. He began to talk to her about how warm it was, HOT even. He asked her, "Have you noticed how hot it is?" She said that she had noticed. He told her that the fire made it even hotter inside the house and that she looked very hot. She replied that she was indeed very hot.

"Why don't you lean out of the window for a cooling breeze?" he asked. She replied that it was a good idea and went to the window. As she leaned out, he jumped over to the fire and, with his wet hands, quickly threw one of the hot stones at her. This made the sko'yo fall out of the window and down the cliff, where she died!

Kasewats then freed the people and gave each one some of the sko'yo's possessions. After this, they left for their homes.

Da hama tas'iteh.

da HA-ma tas-ee-TEH

Peggy Garcia, ACOMA

How the Seasons Came to Be

SHAKAK, RULER OF NORTH MOUNTAIN and the spirit of winter, was married to Yellow Woman of the Corn Maidens, who was a daughter of the Acoma chief. They lived together at a place called White House. It was always cold there and no one could plant anything. The people ate only cactus.

One day when Yellow Woman was looking for cactus to gather, she wandered far from her home. In this wandering, she met Miochin. "Why do you gather cactus?" he asked. "Do you not prefer corn or squash or melons?" She told him that such fine foods were not to be found at her home, for such things would not grow there.

As they spoke, she noticed his fine clothes. His shirt was made of woven cornsilk, his belt of green corn leaves. His hat was corn leaves with corn tassels. He had leggings of moss and moccasins embroidered with butterflies. He offered her the green corn he was carrying in his arms. Accepting the gift, she asked where it came from.

"From my home to the south," he replied.

When she returned to her village, she related the meeting to her parents and showed them the wonderful green corn she had been given. They knew that she had met Miochin, the spirit of summer. They asked her to go to the south again the next day and bring him back with her.

Shakak had been hunting. When he came home the next day, he arrived in a swirl of hail and sleet. He knew someone was in his village and in his house. So he called out, "Show yourself!" Miochin stepped out from the next room to see Shakak standing there in his icicle clothing. They agreed to meet in four days to battle over Yellow Woman.

Miochin assembled the birds and animals of summer. Shakak called the birds and animals of winter. On the fourth day they met. Miochin rode in on clouds of steam and smoke. Shakak arrived in a great blizzard. They fought for many hours, but Shakak's weapons of sleet, snow, and hail began to melt, and he had to agree that he had lost the battle.

Miochin then declared that they should share the year henceforth, but

his Spring and Summer would last longer than Shakak's Fall and Winter.
And it has been that way since.

Da hama tas'iteh.

da HA-ma tas-ee-TEH

Dorothy Herrera, COCHITI

The Twins

AN OLD COUPLE LIVED IN THIS VILLAGE. They had never had a child, but they always prayed that some day they would. One morning, after they had offered the sun a morning prayer and corn meal for the day's blessings, they heard a baby cry. They didn't know if it was a trick or if it was real. Then it cried again. But they could not tell where the sound came from. So the old man went north to look, and the old woman went south to look. Each found a baby and came back, exclaiming, "Look what I found!"

They felt certain that someone would be coming to look for the lost babies, so they went to the leader for advice. The leader told them, "You must wait four days. Then, if no one comes forth to claim these babies as family, they are yours."

Four days came and passed and no one came. The old man and the old woman were very happy. The people of the village were happy, too, because the old couple had good hearts, and now, in their old age, they would at last have children. And the children would some day care for the old people.

The twin boys, for that was what they were, grew fast, very fast—much faster than normal children. And they learned all that the old man and the old woman could teach them. They played only with each other and not with the other children of the village. It was said that they ate flowers, danced with butterflies, and spoke with the animals.

The twins dreamed many things, and from these dreams they learned much that no others in the village knew. The old man and the old woman knew these were special children and sent them on a journey to a certain sacred place. After four days the twins returned. They were fully grown and painted in black and white stripes, with corn husks in their hair. As the people came out to see them, the twins began to entertain the villagers. They teased, they laughed, and they clowned. And the people laughed.

A powerful witch-man who lived in the village heard the laughter, and this angered him. The people were afraid of him for he had caused the crops to fail and children to die when he was angered. The witch-man tried to hurt the twins, but he could not. They had great power, too, and had learned many more new things during their journey.

The witch-man challenged them to a contest. He told them that the one who lost must leave the village and give up his life. The twins accepted the challenge.

The twins fasted and prayed, and in four days they were ready. On that day the witch-man brought a large pottery jar into the plaza and sat it down, upside down. Then he placed it upright and commanded the water to flow. Water overflowed the jar, running like a river, nearly filling up the plaza before suddenly disappearing. Then corn and beans and squash appeared, growing, flowering, and ripening right before the eyes of the people. Then the growing things withered and disappeared.

The twins praised him for his skills and power, and in spite of himself, the witch-man was flattered. The twins said to him, "Too bad that you couldn't make it last. All those good things disappeared." The people laughed and the witch-man became angry, screaming, "Begin!" And they did.

One twin turned toward the other and said, "Little-Brother-Before-Me, go bring some ashes that I might make a cloud."

"I will, Little-Brother-Before-Me," said the other, though of course no one could know which twin came first. When the brother returned and handed the ashes to the other, the twin took them and blew on them. It caused his brother to sneeze and cough and the people to laugh. But no clouds came. Then the other twin came and took the remaining ashes and threw them into the air. They came down, grey, all over their hair. The people laughed, but still no clouds appeared. The twins made the people laugh, even though they were afraid of what would happen if the witch-man won. The witch was deeply angry, but he waited.

Finally, one twin began to talk. Then the other. They talked quietly, then more quietly. Everyone grew especially quiet and listened. They lis-

Karen Tenorio, SANTO DOMINGO

tened very carefully. The twins talked about the clouds they had seen. They talked about rainbows. They spoke of thunder and lightning. They talked about the fresh smell of wet earth and the green things that grow soon after the rain. And pretty soon one twin blew in his cupped hands and a cloud arose and grew large. Very large. Soon it was raining! Then it began to thunder and flash lightning. It rained harder, and everyone ran happily into their homes.

When they came out of their houses the next morning, they found the witch-man dead from the lightning. The twins were the first Kossa and became the leaders of the village for many good years.

KOS-sah
Kossa, also known as Koshare or Koyala, are sacred clowns who appear in the ceremonies of many of the Rio Grande and Hopi villages.

Buffy Cordero, COCHITI

Snowflake Flower, Cochiti
(Stephanie Rhoades)

A Man Learns to Believe

SHEE-pap

THERE WAS A MAN IN THE VILLAGE who had never believed in the ceremonies. Or in living again after death in the Shipap. He never believed there was Shipap, where the people came from and where they return. He never danced or took part in the ceremonies or helped in any way. Whenever he saw an insect, he crushed it. He tore down the nests of birds and then ate the eggs. He threw rocks at snakes and killed them.

One day he found some eggs in a nest. He made holes in the ends and sucked them dry. When he came back to the village, he sat outside his house, resting after his meal. The people suddenly heard a great sound. Like a whip, a snake flew through the air and into the man's mouth. He had eaten the snake's eggs! The man fell over, and everyone ran way. The snake came out of his mouth, carrying its eggs, and slithered away. When the people of the village came back, the man was dead.

So the people prepared to bury him. The priest of the Shipap knew of this man and knew of his death. He immediately sent messengers to bring the dead man's spirit to Shipap. The messengers took his spirit and returned along the road they had come. As they went, the man's spirit marveled at how clear the road was. He saw how beautiful the fields were.

There were beautiful green corn, yellow melons, and young green bean plants.

"How is it that these places we pass have come to be this beautiful?" the man asked.

"It is because the people who care for the fields and use the roads to bring the water believe and have good hearts," replied the messengers.

Presently they arrived at Shipap. He was taken to a room. The headmen were all there, and they were very sad. They were sad for all the things that this man had done and what he had not done. Sorrow lay on their hearts because this man had not believed and lived with a good heart. The man's spirit saw this and wept.

The headman told him he could go back to his body, that it was not too late if he hurried, but, they counseled, "You must believe in everything!"

To this he readily agreed, agreeing with his whole heart. The messengers hurried him to his village and hurled him back into his body. When he awoke he embraced his father and embraced his mother, and they were very happy. He told them what the headman had told him and what he was instructed to do. "They told me not to harm snakes or insects or birds or any of our brothers. They told me that when I am hunting, I must respect the spirits of those that let themselves be taken. They told me to believe in the katsinas and listen to the medicine men. They told me to believe in everything."

And he always did after that, and he grew very old, and he became a cacique who served the people well.

ka-SEEK keh

Clay Old Woman and Clay Old Man

Ik'tinaku made Clay Old Woman and Clay Old Man. She sent them to Kot'yeteh (Cochiti). Clay Old Woman went into the plaza and sat down. She had brought clay and water and sand with her. She began to mix them. When she finished mixing, she rolled it into a ball and wrapped it in a piece of white cloth.

EK-tee-nah-koo

When she was ready, she took the ball and began to coil a pot from it. Clay Old Man was dancing and singing while she worked. All the people gathered around to watch. They watched all day and listened to Clay Old Man sing while he danced. But while he was dancing, he kicked over one of her pots and broke it. Clay Old Woman became very angry and chased the old man all around the plaza with a stick. But then they made up and she started her pottery making again. She took the broken pieces and soaked them in water and rolled them back into a ball of clay. Clay Old Man took pieces of that clay and gave some to everyone in the village. Everyone began to coil pots like they had seen Clay Old Woman.

And that is how we learned to make pottery. Clay Old Woman and Clay Old Man told us never to forget to make pottery.

Zuni Pueblo

Zuni is a Spanish version of the name given them by the Keresan-speaking pueblos. They call themselves Ashiwi (AH-she-wee) and give the name Itiwana, or 'the Middle Place,' for their pueblo, although Halonawa and Shiwina are sometimes used.

The Zuni, by their own account in their Chimiky'ana'kowa (creation and emergence story) and according to archaeological evidence, are a mix of at least two groups, one from the north and the other from the south. Their language is unrelated to that of any other tribe in the Southwest.

Before the Spanish arrived, there were over 3,000 Zuni living in six villages in their broad valley. The present village, located southwest of Gallup, New Mexico, is built on the site of one of these earlier villages. The Spanish explorer Fray Marcos de Niza believed that the villages were the Seven Cities of Cíbola. De Niza's guide, Esteban, was killed at Zuni for his insulting behavior, so de Niza viewed the pueblos from a safe distance, declared them to be the fabled cities, and returned to Mexico. Based on de Niza's glowing report, Francisco Coronado returned the following year with a group of soldiers, only to find the villages were made of stone and earth, not gold. The present village, built in 1662, and its surrounding 400,000 acres are home to most of the tribe's 9,000 members.

A modest pottery revival at Zuni has kept the craft alive. The pueblo is still best known for its jewelry of stone and shell set in silver.

ZUNI

Beaded Storyteller

Nellie Bika, ZUNI

Owl

The Boy Outwits the Bear

sohn-AH-chee

SON'ACHEE.

A MAIDEN WAS MARRIED TO A GOD OF THE RAIN. Together they had a son. He grew very rapidly and in a few months was as a child of six or seven years. Each day he would hunt birds around the edge of the village. Using only his hands and stones, he always managed to catch many birds. But he saw that the older boys and men carried bows and arrows with which they could slay much larger birds, including turkeys. He wished to have such weapons also and asked his mother, "Where do the sticks grow for arrows, and where does the wood for bows grow?"

She did not want to tell him because she did not want him to leave the village and go where harm might come to him. But he persisted, asking and tugging at her dress. At last she told him, but warned that it was a dangerous place. There was an old and ugly bear living nearby who had devoured many who had ventured there. The boy promised not to go, but that very night he lay on his sleeping mat, making plans to go to find the bear the very next morning.

Before dawn he slipped away from the village. Following his mother's description, he found the place when the sun was high above him. Far up on a cliff he saw a cave. Before gathering the wood and sticks, he looked out over the valley for the bear. As he stood there, his Rain Father gathered clouds and threw a bolt of lightning, closing the cave for a moment in order to warn the boy against entering. Rain Father did this four times and then said, "He ignores my advice just as he ignores the advice of his mother. Our words are just the wind in his ears. He must go his own way and learn."

So saying, he left, and the boy turned and stepped inside the cave. Instantly there was a fierce growl as the bear stood up and grabbed the boy in powerful arms, pinning him with his great claws. The terrified boy spoke quickly, telling the bear, "My mother is very beautiful and good. If you release me, my mother will happily marry you."

This pleased the ugly bear greatly! The bear not only let him go, but agreed to show him how to make arrows and fashion a bow. He even gathered the wood and sticks for the youth, so anxious was he to favorably impress his wife-to-be. Handing the boy the wood, he told him, "I will be at your village near sunset tomorrow to see how well you have made the bow, how straight the arrows are, and to claim my bride."

The boy hailed his mother as he entered the village, "I am back from where the bear lives, with the wood and sticks for my bow and arrows!"

"Ungrateful son, how is it that the bear did not harm you?" his mother asked.

"I promised the bear that you would be his wife," he replied. "But do not fear, I have a plan."

The next morning he began to work very hard and skillfully on his bow and arrows. He worked all day. The bear had mentioned nothing about how to fashion arrow points, but the boy chipped hard, sharp points of black obsidian.

At sunset the bear strolled into the village and came straight up the house ladder where the boy and his mother lived. "Have you made the bow and arrows, my son?" he asked.

"As best as I could," the boy answered modestly.

The bear tested the bow and murmured his approval. Then he looked at the arrows and exclaimed, "But what is this on the end? Coal?"

"No," said the boy. "They are black obsidian, as good and as hard and as sharp as any flint point!"

"Coal!" growled the bear, unaccustomed to having anyone disagree with him. "Coal and worthless!" he bellowed.

"Then I shall prove it," cried the boy, and he snatched up an arrow and fit it to his bow. Before the bear could move, the boy let fly the arrow straight into the bear's heart, passing completely through him. The bear fell dead.

The boy then skinned the bear and hung the heart from the top of their house ladder, that others might know he had slain the bear and that now it was safe to venture forth for wood for bows and arrows.

Semonyika.   see-MON-yee-kah

Hopi Pueblos

The Hopi speak a Uto-Aztecan language related to that spoken by other tribes south of them and on into Mexico. The Hopi number 9,000 members, with many living off the 1,600,000-acre reservation. The Hopi Reservation is completely encircled by the much larger Navajo Reservation. They have lived for many centuries on this high, arid plateau with its short growing season. Though the area is dotted with ruins of older sites, the oldest continually occupied village is Oraibi (oh-RAH-bee), founded about 1150 A.D. One village, Hano, was settled by Tewa Indians from the Rio Grande Valley after the Great Pueblo Revolt of 1680. Its members speak both Hopi and Tewa but maintain the Tewa religion and customs.

When the Spanish arrived in 1540, there were seven independent villages, each with its own religious leader, who also handled secular matters. There are now twelve villages, but while each New Mexican pueblo enjoys self-government, the federal government insists on treating the autonomous Hopi villages as a single unit. The tribal council concept was forced upon the Hopi in the middle of this century and has been a source of factionalism.

The Hopi create a wide range of crafts, including silver jewelry, several types of basketry and pottery, katsina carvings, and a limited amount of weaving and embroidery.

Laura Waterfox, HOPI
Koshare

Laura Waterfox, HOPI
Mudhead

The Man Who Was Married to a Witch

ah-LEEK-sah-ai

ALIKSA-AI.

AT ORAIBI VILLAGE THERE LIVED A COUPLE WHO HAD NO CHILDREN. The husband was a very hard worker. In the summer he went to work in his fields every day. One day when he returned, he smelled a delicious smell—mutton stew! As he was very hungry, he was anxious to sit down and eat such good food. But when his wife served the dinner, there was no delicious mutton stew—only a thin corn soup. This happened many times after that, and so he began to wonder what his wife did with the stew she made but never gave to him.

One evening after dinner, he was thinking very hard about this. While he was thinking, his wife kept asking him to come to sleep. Finally he did, but he only pretended to be asleep. After awhile his wife poked him. Then she poked him again, harder, to see if he was really asleep. The husband knew this and just lay there, still pretending to be asleep. Satisfied that he was sleeping, she bundled some corn cobs up in a blanket next to him so he would think she was still there, and then she left. As soon as he heard her go out, he jumped up and followed her. He followed her far to the west to a place he had never noticed before. When she entered that place he heard people greet her, saying, "You are late. We have been waiting."

She answered them saying, "My husband went to sleep late this evening so I could not come before now. Let us begin our business." She said this, for she was the leader of these people.

A hoop was set up in the middle of the room. One person passed through it and said, "Nothing happened! Something is wrong!"

And so it was until after the fourth person had tried and still nothing happened. The woman said, "Someone must be watching us!" And they all rushed outside to look. They quickly found and caught the poor husband, but they acted very nice, saying, "Don't stay outside, come in and join us." He had no choice.

Then they began again. This time, when the people passed through the hoop, things happened. Each one was changed into a bird or an animal of the night, like bats, coyotes, and owls. And as they changed, they went out into the night. While they were gone the husband was sitting and thinking, and he realized that this was where she had brought the stew she made each evening and did not serve to him.

About this time the people came back, passing through the hoop and changing back into human form. They gathered about and began a strange ceremony. The man had never seen the dance or heard the songs before. Though he tried to watch and listen, he feel asleep.

When he awoke, he found himself alone on a narrow ledge. Below him a cliff wall stretched many hundred feet to the ground. Above him the wall was just as smooth and high. The ledge was so narrow he did not dare to move.

The man was worried and unhappy. "Because I followed my wife, this happened to me," he said. As he lay there, a wren landed on him and spoke, "I have come to help you, but first you must resist two who are coming. They will try to make you fall from the ledge by tossing food down for you to catch. You must not try to catch it or you will surely fall. I shall come back to see what has happened." Then the wren flew off.

Before he could even wonder about the wren's warning, he heard voices. They were coming from above him. Pretty soon two faces appeared at the edge of the cliff.

"You seem to be in a terrible fix," said one.

"You must be very hungry," said the other.

"We will toss you some nice sweet baked corn," said the first, "You must catch it and eat it."

So saying, they began to toss him some corn. But remembering the wren's instructions, he did not try to catch any. Finally they ran out of corn and left.

When the wren returned, it said, "You did well, but soon you will have another test. A creature will come to throw you off the cliff. You must not move. I will give you some medicine that you must spit on the creature when it gets close enough. If you survive, I will be back to help you." And again he flew off.

Before the sun was directly overhead, the man heard some sounds from the cliff's edge. The sounds continued and came closer. Whatever it was, it was coming down the cliff straight towards him! He looked up the cliff to see a monstrous snake slowly slithering down the cliff to his tiny ledge. The man held back his fear as the snake drew closer and closer. Finally when it was about to touch him, he spit the wren's medicine on its head. The snake cried out and plummeted past him to the base of the cliff far below.

The wren flew back and said, "It is good. Now I shall take you down from this place." It flew down to the bottom of the cliff and spit its medicine on the base, causing a crack to appear all the way up to where the man lay. Then the wren began to pluck its feathers, sticking them into the rock one at a time. In doing so, it made its way up to the man, but by that time, the bird was bald!

The wren said to the man, "Do not be afraid. Climb on my back and shut your eyes very tight until we are on the ground and I tell you to open them, or you will surely fall and die." The man did as he was told and down the cliff they went, slowly and steadily.

After a time the wren said, "Now we are down and you may open your eyes. You may go back to your people and to your home. But when you get there, do not be angry when you see your wife and she seems happy to see you. She will be at an end soon enough."

Indeed, when he went home his wife acted as though nothing had happened and she was happy to have him. The next morning his wife began to act very crazy and to move jerkily towards the edge of the mesa. At the edge, she stumbled and fell over the cliff and died. So, too, did the other witches come to an end.

pai YOOK poo-lah   Pai yook puhluh.

Coyote Eyes

Aliksa-ai.

Skeleton lived near Coyote Woman. Coyote Woman lived near Skeleton. One time when Coyote Woman was hunting, she saw Skeleton going to a place where he sometimes danced. Since Coyote Woman was always more curious than she should be, she went nearer. Skeleton began to sing after awhile. Because he was a skeleton, he had no eyes, only eye sockets. Yet when he began to sing his songs, eyes came out of his sockets! The eyes traveled to the south. Even though Skeleton stayed where he was, he was able to see through those eyes as they traveled. Pretty soon the eyes were past the mesas, past the desert, and had entered a canyon near the mountains. There they saw a stream, a fine meadow, and much game. Coyote Woman knew this, for Skeleton spoke as he saw things, saying "What a fine place. What a fat deer! That is a nice stream!" Coyote Woman grew very envious.

Finally Skeleton began to sing again. And presently his eyes reappeared in the distance, traveling toward him, finally arriving and jumping back into the empty sockets. Coyote Woman decided she wanted to learn how to do this, but as usual, instead of just asking, she tried to flatter and out-smart Skeleton.

"That was a very fine song you were singing," said Coyote Woman as she walked up to Skeleton from where she had been sitting and watching.

Skeleton only nodded.

"If I knew such a fine song I could sing it with my beautiful voice for others to enjoy," she bragged. Skeleton pretended not to hear.

"I would be honored to learn from someone such as you. Besides, I am used to handling such song magic," she said.

So Skeleton agreed to teach Coyote Woman the song. As soon as she had learned the song she wanted to go traveling with her eyes. "You must first stand over there," said Skeleton, motioning to the side of the arroyo, "and face south. When you are ready for them to return, just sing them back and they will come!" Saying this, Skeleton left.

ah-LEEK-sah-ai

Coyote Woman ran right over to the spot he had pointed out and began to dance and sing. Loudly. Pretty soon her eyes popped right out and began traveling south, as Skeleton's eyes had. Soon she was seeing the same things that Skeleton had seen. Before long it began to get dark, and she decided she'd better call her eyes back and go home. She began to sing, but her eyes did not return.

"Oh, dear," she said. "I'd better sing again, for it is dark and they have not arrived!"

Again she sang, but still her eyes did not come back, for she was no longer facing south!

"Something is wrong," she wailed. "Perhaps they have arrived and are lying on the ground." So saying, she began to search nearby for them. In a few minutes she found a round object with a cord attached and popped it into one eye socket. This helped her find another, which she quickly put into the other socket.

"This is very strange," she said. "Everything is quite yellow. Well, I must hurry home. I will figure this out in the morning. Perhaps it is just the last light of the day that is making everything look yellow."

Hidden nearby, Skeleton was laughing, for Coyote Woman had stuck two yellow gourds in her eye sockets. When she arrived home, her pups saw her strange and terrifying yellow eyes. They screamed in fright and fled in all directions. Poor Coyote Woman tried to call them back, but they didn't come.

And that is why coyotes live everywhere nowadays.

pai YOOK poo-lah   Pai yook puhluh.

Navajo Traditions

Although not a Pueblo people, the Navajo (who call themselves Diné, meaning `The People') also have a strong and ancient oral tradition. Currently their 205,000 members live on a 17-million-acre reservation that encompasses much of the Four Corners area of Arizona, New Mexico, Colorado, and Utah.

dee-NEH

Related to the Apache, the Navajo reached the Southwest shortly after 1000 AD. Their culture has been influenced by their proximity to the Pueblo peoples. A nomadic people, the Navajo were composed of a great number of independent bands. Despite this, the American government attempted to enforce agreements signed by only one or two headmen. As Navajo raids continued, the military began a scorched earth policy in 1863 that ultimately brought most of the Navajo to defeat and imprisonment in southern New Mexico. The Navajo were not allowed to return home until 1868.

The Navajo are best known for their silverwork and exceptional weaving. Pottery-making has undergone a revival in the last twenty years. Though many potters create a range of animal figurines, neither human figurines in general nor storyteller figures in particular are often made.

Betty Manygoats, NAVAJO

Cheyenne Jim, NAVAJO

Slaying the Monsters

CHANGING WOMAN HAD TWO SONS, Nayenezgani, meaning Monster Slayer, and Tobaschin, meaning Born of Water. Many yei-tso, or monsters, inhabited the world, making it unsafe for the people. The Twins set about finding and killing each of the monsters.

They first went after the Horned Monster. When they found it and it saw them, the monster charged. The Twins stood very still until it was very close. Then they threw four flint knives at it. All four knives struck it in the head, but still it came and did not die until it reached them.

When they went home to their mother to tell her of what had happened, they learned that a Monster Eagle was catching and eating the people. People tried to sneak past him, but he had many other birds who were always watching and told Monster Eagle when a new victim was near. The Twins hid themselves in a summer haze until they were quite near the Monster Eagle's nest. When it saw them, Monster Eagle rose up and dove down, catching Monster Slayer and dropping him in its nest. Then it went after Born of Water. While it was gone, Monster Slayer killed the young monsters in the nest and threw them over the side. When Monster Eagle arrived with Born of Water, Monster Slayer rose up and shot it with lightning. Born of Water then stabbed it with his great flint knife, and Monster Eagle fell dead at the base of the cliff.

And so they killed many of the monsters, but some asked the Twins to spare their lives. Among these were Old Age and Death. They explained, "Please do not kill us. We have not harmed anyone. Without us the old ones will not die and the young ones will not grow up. It is well that your people should grow old. Then they pass away and give their places to the young." Monster Slayer thought about this and decided Old Age and Death should be allowed to live.

Another allowed to live was Poverty. Poverty was an old man and an old woman who were dirty and wore tattered clothes. They owned nothing. "Do not kill us," they pleaded. "It would not be wise. When the people's clothes wear out, they must make new ones. They will have to work.

nah-YEN-nez-gah-nee

toe-BAH-sheen

Let us live so that they must work hard. It will be good and they will not become lazy."

The Twins then went to kill Lice. But Lice, too, asked that they reconsider killing him and his family. "We itch and bother people, it is true. But you must let us live because we remind the people to keep themselves clean." Next came Hunger. Hunger was an old, thin, bony man. "You would be foolish to kill me," he croaked. "Without me the people would not know the rewards of hunting and of planting. I remind them of the importance of such work."

And so it was that the Twins agreed that certain monsters were necessary and would be allowed to live. And so it is that Hunger, Poverty, Lice, Old Age, and Death are still among us.

Suggested Reading List

Applegate, Frank G. *Indian Stories from the Pueblos*. Glorieta, NM: RioGrande Press, 1982.

>   First published in 1929, there is quite a range of stories included, written in a style that the original foreword describes as "homely and vivid."

Babcock, Barbara A. *The Pueblo Storyteller: Development of a Figurative Tradition*. Tucson: University of Arizona Press, 1986.

>   An excellent book on the Pueblo figurative tradition in general and storyteller figurines in particular. Profusely illustrated and filled with detailed information, including an extensive listing of storyteller makers and their pueblos.

Bahti, Tom. *Southwestern Indian Ceremonials*. Las Vegas, NV: K.C. Publications, 1970.

_____. *Southwestern Indian Tribes* (Revised edition, 1996). Las Vegas, NV: K.C. Publications, 1984.

>   These two classic volumes provide an excellent overview of the history and religions of the Southwestern tribes, along with an extensive reading list.

Vera Fragua, JEMEZ

Baylor, Byrd. *And It Is Still That Way: Legends Told By Arizona Indian Children*. New York: Scribners, 1976.
These are stories that children have heard and retold to Byrd Baylor, who wisely let them speak for themselves.

_____. *A God on Every Mountain Top*. New York: Scribners, 1976.
Nicely illustrated by Carol Brown, this is not for children only. More poetry than prose, these are lyrical re-tellings of Indian legends about mountains.

Benedict, Ruth. *Tales of the Cochiti Indians*. Albuquerque, NM: University of New Mexico Press, 1981.
Santiago Quintana, grandfather of Helen Cordero, helped Ruth Benedict record many of these stories, collected in 1924.

Cushing, Frank Hamilton. *Zuni Folk Tales*. Tucson: University of Arizona Press, 1986.
First published in 1901, this book is written in the style of the day, described by some as stilted and by others as stately.

Evers, Larry, ed. *The South Corner of Time: Hopi, Navajo, Papago, and Yaqui Tribal Literature*. Tucson: University of Arizona Press, 1981.
Old stories and new writings by Indian authors along with some very fine black and white photo essays.

Evers, Larry, and Ofelia Zepeda, eds. *Home Places*. Tucson: Sun Tracks and University of Arizona Press, 1995.
Contemporary Indian poems, songs, and stories.

Hausman, Gerald. *The Gift of the Gila Monster*. New York: Simon & Schuster, 1993.
A collection of Navajo stories from the religious healing rites used to restore the patient to harmony or balance.

James, Ahlee. *Tewa Firelight Tales*. New York: Longmans, Green and Co., 1927.
Though long out of print, this book contains versions of a number of stories and is illustrated by several Tewa Indian artists.

Malotki, Ekkehart. *Hopitutuwutsi/Hopi Tales*. Tucson: University of
Arizona Press, 1983.
    An excellent bilingual collection of Hopi stories. Nicely illustrated,
    unfortunately also out of print.

_____. *Gullible Coyote/Una'ihu*. Tucson: University of Arizona
Press, 1986.
    A very well done collection of bilingual stories from the Hopi, with
    illustrations.

Nequatewa, Edmund. *Truth of a Hopi: Stories Relating to the Origin,
Myths and Clan Histories of the Hopi*. Flagstaff, AZ: Northland Press, 1973.
    The author is a traditional Hopi from the village of Hotevilla. The title
    says it all.

Ortiz, Simon J., ed. *Earth Power Coming*. Tsaile, AZ: Navajo Community
College Press, 1983.
    Outstanding contemporary short fiction by Indian writers.

Parsons, Elsie Clew. *Tewa Tales*. Tucson: University of Arizona Press, 1994.
    A reprint of an old collection of tales.

Rock Point Community School. *Between Sacred Mountains: Navajo Stories
and Lessons from the Land*. Tucson: Sun Tracks and University of Arizona
Press, 1984.
    A compilation of stories about the Navajo people and their land by
    the Navajos themselves.

Roessel, Robert A., Jr., and Dillon Platero, eds. *Coyote Stories of the
Navajo People*. Phoenix, AZ: Navajo Curriculum Center Press, 1974.
    Alhough originally written for Navajo children, non-Navajos of all
    ages will find it interesting.

Tedlock, Dennis. *Finding the Center: Narrative Poetry of the Zuni Indians*.
Lincoln: University of Nebraska Press, 1972.
    Without a doubt the finest book currently available for those who
    wish to understand the richness and depth of traditional Pueblo oral
    traditions, with an invaluable introduction.

Velarde, Pablita. *Old Father the Storyteller.* (new edition) Santa Fe, NM: Clearlight Press, 1989.

This finely illustrated book by an outstanding artist from Santa Clara Pueblo, originally published in 1960, is happily back in print.

The Zuni People. *Self-Portrayals.* Albuquerque: University of New Mexico Press, 1972.

Containing a range of stories about the Zuni, this was one of the first books about a tribe written by that tribe.

Dorothy Herrera, Cochiti

Detail